HELP ME — I'M INSECURE!

**Overcoming Emotional Battles
With the Power of God's Word**

by

Joyce Meyer

Harrison House
Tulsa, Oklahoma

HELP ME — I'M INSECURE!
Overcoming Emotional Battles
With the Power of God's Word
ISBN 1-57794-042-3
Copyright © 1998 by Joyce Meyer
Life In The Word, Inc.
P. O. Box 655
Fenton, Missouri 63026

Published by Harrison House, Inc.
P. O. Box 35035
Tulsa, Oklahoma 74153

Contents

Introduction

Are you tired of playing games, wearing masks, trying to be someone other than who you are? Wouldn't you like the freedom just to be accepted as you are, without pressure to be someone you really don't know how to be?

Would you like to learn how to succeed at being yourself?

God wants us to accept ourselves, to like who we are and to learn to deal with our weaknesses because we all have plenty of them. He doesn't want us to reject ourselves because of them.

Jesus understands our weaknesses. (Hebrews 4:15.)

The Holy Spirit bears us up in our weakness. (Romans 8:26.)

God chooses weak and foolish things of the world to confound the wise. (1 Corinthians 1:27.)

If I look at my weaknesses and tell you what I believe my value is, it will be less than nothing. But our worth is not based on anything we do but in what God has already done.

God accepts us as we are, but the devil tries very hard to keep us from really understanding that. He brings pressure on us from many different sources to try to keep us feeling we don't measure up to the standard of where we should be. He doesn't want us to find out we can accept and like ourselves just as we are because he knows if we ever do that, something wonderful will begin happening to us.

The opinion we have of ourself affects all our relationships — with people and with God. Because it affects our relationship with God, it affects our prayer life.

We can pray and pray, basing our prayers on the promises God gives us in the Scriptures and using all the right words, without the prayer being effective. One reason the prayer may not bear fruit is if we have such bad feelings about ourselves we don't believe God ought to do for us what we are asking. We have a hard time praying and believing God will do the great thing we are praying about because we don't expect Him to do it! We base our own value on our performance letting our weaknesses, flaws and failures negatively affect our opinion of ourselves.

People are extremely performance oriented. We learn from the time we are little, the better we perform the more love we receive. In our relationship with God, our thinking often continues in this pattern. We think God will love us and bless us more, the better we perform. But because we aren't able to behave right all the time, we start working and striving, trying to overcome all our weaknesses. We think God will then love us enough to do for us what we need.

Our worth is not in what *we* do, but in what God has made us through what *He* has done. Every Christian knows this principle — it is the basis of salvation. We are made righteous, or put in rightstanding with God, through what Jesus did by dying on the cross. We cannot earn salvation by what *we* do — it is a free gift from God because of what *Jesus* did. (1 Corinthians 1:30; Ephesians 2:8.) We just need to accept it.

But even though every Christian received salvation by believing we are made right with God through what He did, usually only very mature Christians continue in this truth and learn to approach all of life on the same basis. (Galatians 3:3.) As we saw, this type of thinking is contrary to the way most people were brought up to think. We must change our thinking by renewing our mind with the Scriptures that teach our rightstanding with God is through Jesus — not through our own works.

Our worth is not based on how acceptable we can make ourselves to God. God is looking for people with a right heart attitude toward Him, not a perfect performance record. Second Chronicles 16:9 (KJV) says,

"For the eyes of the LORD run to and fro throughout the whole earth, to shew himself strong in the behalf of them whose heart is perfect toward him...."

"...whose heart is perfect toward him," means to have a right heart attitude toward God — to love God as much as we know how to love Him; to want what He wants; to want His will; to want to do His will.

God has made the provision for us to be in rightstanding with Him (if we will accept it). He loves us and is looking for people who are open to His will so that He can show Himself strong in their behalf and bless them.

We don't earn God's love; we don't earn His blessings. We can go to Him at anytime and have our needs met. Hebrews 4:16 says, "Let us then fearlessly and confidently and boldly draw near to the throne of grace (the throne of God's unmerited favor to us sinners), that we may receive mercy [for our failures] and find grace to help in good time for every need [appropriate help and well-timed help, coming just when we need it]."

However, the ongoing lifestyle we choose affects our ability to receive all that God has for us. A life of serving and obeying God allows Him to place us in a position for Him to open several avenues to use in consistently blessing us. Faithfulness releases blessings. (Proverbs 28:20.)

A lifestyle of disobedience will definitely affect what God is able to do in our lives because the Bible teaches if we plant bad seeds, we will reap a bad harvest. (Galatians 6:8.)

People who live and walk in intentional disobedience, but want God to bless them anyway, may think that we don't have to make an effort to overcome our weaknesses to win God's approval. They believe if we are weak in an area, we have an excuse to sin. The truth is this: God will use us in spite of our weaknesses and will help us overcome them; we don't have to struggle to overcome them on our own, but we must be progressing toward overcoming them.

The Lord told Paul: "...My strength and power are made perfect (fulfilled and completed) and show themselves most effective in [your] weakness..." (2 Corinthians 12:9). Second Corinthians 13:4 (KJV) tells us we are "...weak in him, but we shall live with him by the power of God...."

When Paul was teaching the Romans the message of grace he said:

> ...Are we to remain in sin in order that God's grace (favor and mercy) may multiply and overflow?
>
> Certainly not! How can we who died to sin live in it any longer?
>
> *Romans 6:1,2*

In other words, should we see how much we can sin because sinning will give God an opportunity to give us grace? Paul's response in so many words was, "For crying out loud — how can you sin if you're dead to sin?"

Paul's point was to teach them who they were in Christ. They and we are acceptable because God made us acceptable. (Romans 6:5-16.)

God wants us to come to terms with ourselves and learn our value is not in what we do but in who we are. He wants us to be willing to be who we are, weaknesses and all.

It's wonderful not to start the day by waking up and hating yourself for half an hour before you ever get out of bed! Or wake up to hear the devil rattling in your ears a list of all the mistakes you made the day before, telling you you're a failure and can't expect God to do anything good for you. Many people are beat down before they ever get their feet on the floor in the morning!

The devil's plan is to deceive us into continuing to base our worth on our performance, then keep us focused on our faults and shortcomings. Satan wants us to have a low opinion of ourselves and be insecure so that we live ineffectively for God, being miserable and unreceptive to God's blessings because we don't think we deserve them.

Once we come into peace with ourselves, we will begin to come into peace with other people. If we ever learn to accept and like ourselves, we will begin to accept and like others. I know from personal experience the more able I am to accept and like myself in spite of my weaknesses and flaws, the more able I am to accept and like others in spite of theirs.

Every one of us is imperfect, and God loves us just the way we are.

By applying the Bible-based principles in this book you will overcome the sense of personal insecurity and will prepare yourself to fulfill God's marvelous plan for your life.

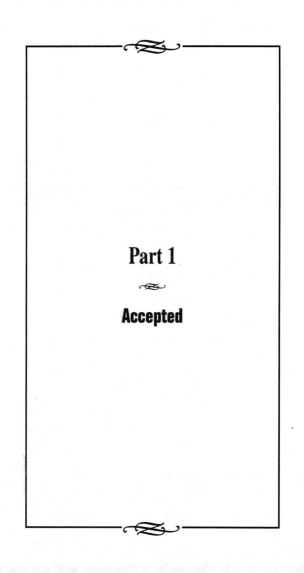

Part 1

Accepted

1

⚛

Eliminate the Negative

If you want to increase your self-acceptance and your opinion of yourself, decide right here and now that not one more negative thing about you will ever come out of your mouth.

Acknowledge the Good Things

That the communication of thy faith may become effectual by the acknowledging of every good thing which is in you in Christ Jesus.

Philemon 1:6 KJV

The communication of our faith is made effectual by acknowledging every *good thing* which is in us *in Christ Jesus,* not by acknowledging every *wrong* thing with *us.*

The devil wants us to acknowledge every bad thing we see in ourselves because he doesn't want the communication of our faith to be effectual. He wants us to spend every waking moment acknowledging in our mind and out of our mouth how awful we are because, as the accuser of the brethren (Revelation 12:9,10), he continually tries to redirect our focus from who we are in Christ back onto our shortcomings.

The devil wants to bombard us with opportunities to think negative thoughts about ourselves so that we will return to that pattern of thinking most of us learned growing up. We will again fall into the deception that our worth is based on our performance, and because of our faults, we are worthless.

One reason it is so important not to speak negatively about ourselves is that we believe what we say more than what anybody else says. But once we truly understand who we are in Christ and see how much He has done for us through shedding His blood to make us worthy, we will realize we are actually insulting our heavenly Father by excessively meditating on our faults, flaws and failures. Acts 10:15 says: "...What God has cleansed and pronounced clean, do not you defile and profane by regarding and calling common and unhallowed or unclean."

In Rightstanding With God

One of the first revelations God gave me out of the Word was on righteousness. By "revelation" I mean one day you suddenly understand something to the point that it becomes part of you. The knowledge isn't only in your mind — you no longer need to renew your mind to it because you don't wonder or hope it's true — you *know*.

I *knew* I was righteous in Christ because God gave me an understanding of 2 Corinthians 5:21:

> For our sake He [God] made Christ [virtually] to be sin Who knew no sin, so that in and through Him

we might become [endued with,
viewed as being in, and examples of]
the righteousness of God [what we
ought to be, approved and acceptable
and in right relationship with Him,
by His goodness].

Righteousness Is God's Gift

Romans 4:24 tells us:

...[Righteousness, standing acceptable to God] will be granted and
credited to us also who believe in (trust
in, adhere to, and rely on) God, Who
raised Jesus our Lord from the dead.

Romans 4:24

I understood that righteousness is something given to us. It is "imputed" (KJV) to us
— "granted and credited" to us by virtue of
our believing in what God did for us through
His Son Jesus Christ. Jesus, Who knew no
sin, became sin so that we might be made the
righteousness of God in Jesus.

Above all else, the devil does not want us to walk in the reality that we are in right-standing with God. He wants us always vaguely contemplating what is wrong with us instead of thinking about what is right with us through Jesus' blood.

I had been walking in this revelation of righteousness for a few years and teaching the Word for quite a while, when something happened that showed me how important it is not to speak negatively about ourselves. When we receive a revelation, we are held responsible for it, and I was held responsible for saying negative things about myself.

The Importance of Speaking in Line With God's Word

Dave and I planned and prayed to have our son Daniel. He wasn't an accident — we wanted him. But after he was born, I let the change in my lifestyle affect me negatively.

I wasn't used to spending so much time in the house. I had put on a few pounds and my skin had gone through changes, normal with having a baby. But I thought I was ugly and fat and would stay that way forever. I fell into a permanent lousy mood.

One morning before Dave left for work, he was trying to encourage and cheer me up. In the process he told me I really should not be acting as I was, that I knew better. I got mad at him. Then he said something else, and I said something else, and at last I had an excuse to do what I had wanted to do for days — blow up.

My background was very negative. I had a negative mouth and a very negative attitude about everything and everybody including myself. When I made mistakes or did things wrong, it was normal for me to think, "I can't ever do anything right — I'm just a big jerk — everything I do is wrong, all the time."

After Dave left and I was alone in the house nursing Daniel at the kitchen table, thinking about what had just happened, I started speaking bad things to myself: "That's right, Joyce, you're just a big jerk. You're a mess. You think studying the Word is going to help you? Nothing's going to help you. You've been a mess as long as you've been on the earth, and you're going to always be a mess. Just forget it; you're never going to straighten up."

All of a sudden I felt an evil, suffocating presence coming across the room at me. It was so strong I could almost see it. From my knowledge of the Word of God, I immediately knew a demonic power was about to attach itself to me because of what I had been saying about myself.

Thank God for the Word we plant in ourselves for without even thinking, I automatically started speaking it out: "*I* am the righteousness of God in Christ. I *am* the righteousness of God in Christ. I am the *righteousness* of God in Christ. I am the righteousness of God in *Christ*. His blood covers me."

In the same way it came in, the evil presence backed off and the atmosphere in the room became clear again. Needless to say, that experience put a holy fear in me about the importance of speaking in line with the Word — especially about myself!

In human beings there is a natural tendency to think negatively. "...the imagination (the strong desire) of man's heart is evil and wicked from his youth..." (Genesis 8:21). This negative tendency will continue until we turn the process around in our life.

God has worked with me since I have been in the Word to change me from being negative and thinking negative thoughts about myself all the time into not thinking or talking like that anymore.

> For as he [a person] thinks in his
> heart, so is he....

Proverbs 23:7

I exhort you to never think or say bad
things about yourself. Your opinion of yourself will make a major difference — in
answered prayer, in what you can receive
from God and in how much God can use
you. God is capable of using you, but you
have to let Him. Let Him by believing He
has made you worthy to receive the good
things He wants to give you. Let Him *by
believing* you are capable of doing what He
asks you to do because *He* will enable you,
and only speak things about yourself in line
with those beliefs.

God's Love Drives Out Insecurity

"We love Him, because He first loved us"
(1 John 4:19). If we don't let God love us,
we are hardly going to be able to love Him
back. If we don't come to some terms of

peace with ourselves, we won't be able to go out and love other people, as the Bible tells us to do: "...You shall love your neighbor as yourself..." (Mark 12:31).

More than anything, people need a revelation of God's love for them personally. God's love for us is the foundation for our faith, for our freedom from sin and for our ability to step out in ministry to others without fear in the form of insecurity.

God made all of us with a craving, longing and desire in our heart to be loved. And the Word teaches us that God loves us as much as He loves Jesus! (See John 17:23.)

People who think their rightstanding with God is based on how much progress they make toward overcoming their flaws think they have worn out God with their failures and messes. We can't wear out God. Love can't be worn out, and we can't cause God not to love us. Love isn't something God does — it is Who He is! (1 John 4:8.)

Many people develop a shame-based nature as a result of unfair and unkind treatment by different people — parents, school teachers, friends, strangers. Our attitudes and our opinions of ourselves are programmed into us over a period of time. If we do not know we are beloved in Christ, we may become insecure. Don't allow how other people treat you to determine your value.

People who lack confidence have a private little war going on within themselves about themselves most of the time. If we focus on the natural world, it isn't difficult to get up every day and start listing the many things wrong with ourselves. The devil puts lies in our heads for us to use in creating a view of ourselves based on what other people say.

Satan Has an Attitude, and He Wants You To Have It!

There is an attitude Satan wants us to have centering on self-dependence. It takes two equally troublesome forms. I don't think he cares which one people choose because both attitudes keep us from the will of God and prevent us from operating in the power available to us as God's children. Both attitudes generate from the belief that our worth is based on self — on us and not God.

A haughty, prideful, self-reliant, self-confident, self-dependent attitude says, "No matter what comes along, I can handle it; I don't need God." Many of us don't think we have this attitude. We say we need God, but this attitude is revealed subtly in our actions. We don't act as though we need God.

As believers we are not to be self-confident but God-confident. The Bible says repeatedly that we are not supposed to have confidence *in ourselves*. Instead, we are to have confidence in God — that He will work *through* us.

People with the other attitude the devil wants us to have condemn themselves. They are angry with themselves over their mistakes and faults. They hate themselves and think they are useless, worthless and ugly. Some people think too highly of themselves and others think too lowly of themselves.

Many people dislike the way they look. They think they are unattractive or are convinced they are ugly when actually they are attractive. The devil is a liar. (John 8:44.) The weapon he has to try to keep us distracted from seeing the truth of who we are and what God has for us is deception. He wants to keep us from fully enjoying the life God has for us and diminish or destroy our effectiveness for God.

One time when I was holding a meeting, the Lord prompted me to ask to come to the front for prayer all those in the audience who felt ugly! I was certainly surprised when He asked me to do that. That was the only time I have ever done that in all the years I have been in ministry.

I said, "Everyone who thinks you're ugly, come up here." The response was enormous!

One girl in the line looked like a fashion model. She was gorgeous. I went to her first because I thought she had misunderstood the altar call.

"Did you understand the invitation was for people who think they're ugly?" I asked.

Tears started streaming down her face as she answered, "All my life I've thought that I was horrible looking." When something happens like that you think, "Do they need glasses or what?" This is a perfect example of the way Satan will deceive. If the devil doesn't keep you busy enough raking yourself over the coals for your weaknesses, he will try to use something that isn't wrong with you or something good about you and make you think it's bad!

God Approves

Before I formed you in the womb
I knew and approved of you [as My

chosen instrument], and before you
were born I separated and set you
apart, consecrating you....

Jeremiah 1:5

God did not create you and me, then say,
"Now I think I'll get to know you." The
Bible says that before He ever formed us in
the womb, He knew us and *approved* of us.

In Ephesians 1:6 (KJV) we are told that
God has made us acceptable in the Beloved.
That means we are made acceptable to God
through the sacrifice of Jesus Christ.

God approved of us before anybody else
ever got a chance to disapprove. If God
approves of us and accepts us as we are, why
worry about what anyone else thinks of us?
If God be for us, who can be against us that
will make any difference? (Romans 8:31.)

Perfection: The Impossible Pursuit

Let no foul or polluting language,
nor evil word nor unwholesome or

worthless talk [ever] come out of your mouth, but only such [speech] as is good and beneficial to the spiritual progress of others, as is fitting to the need and the occasion, that it may be a blessing and give grace (God's favor) to those who hear it.

Ephesians 4:29

My son Danny was playing golf with my husband Dave and me by the time he was nine years old. He was already a good golfer at that age, but he had one serious problem. He had a tendency to be happy when he was playing really well, but if he hit a bad shot he would get upset and start calling himself names. He would say things to himself like, "Oh, stupo Danny, you do everything wrong!"

He felt if he couldn't do everything perfectly, then he was no good at all. If he didn't do everything just right, he began making negative remarks about himself. The devil tried to strap the self-condemnation attitude on Danny at that early age!

Dave and I began working with him, teaching him that was a dangerous habit.

"Danny," we would say, "saying things like that about yourself does not do you any good at all. Nor does it benefit anybody who is with you when you say such things."

This applies to all of us. Not only do we feel bad when we speak negatively about ourselves, but other people hearing someone talk negatively about themselves feel bad. In the verse following the one in which Paul warns us not to allow polluting language or worthless talk to come out of our mouth, he states, "And do not grieve the Holy Spirit of God..." (Ephesians 4:30). Obviously, such negativism grieves the Holy Spirit. It also grieves our own spirit. God has not built us to speak or receive negativism. That's why none of us wants to be around somebody who is always negative.

If a person who makes a mistake says, "I'm not happy about making the mistake, but I'm learning; I'll do better next time; thank God I'm doing as well as I am able," then everybody is edified. The person feels right about himself, and so do others around him. He is taking responsibility for his wrong action without being negative or feeling condemned. That's the attitude and action we should take.

To teach Danny not to speak negative things about himself, the next time I hit a bad shot, I thought, "Well, now I'm going to act the way he's been acting and see if he realizes how silly it is to be that way."

I started saying, "Oh, stupo Joyce, you know, you just never do anything right." Danny didn't even hear me. I tried to say it again, but it was distasteful to me even though I didn't really mean it. Just speaking those words out of my mouth and hearing them in my ears saddened my spirit.

—31—

The Power Is in Our Mouth

For by your words you will be justi-
fied and acquitted, and by your words
you will be condemned and sentenced.

Matthew 12:37

If we speak badly about ourselves, we will
feel condemned. Let's actively apply what
Jesus taught in the Scripture above to speak
positively about ourselves as the first step to
overcoming insecurity, and *never speak negatively about yourself.* Speak words that
empower you — not words that weaken you.

Press Toward the Mark

I do not consider, brethren, that I
have captured and made it my own
[yet]; but one thing I do [it is my one
aspiration]: forgetting what lies
behind and straining forward to
what lies ahead,

I press on toward the goal to win
the [supreme and heavenly] prize to

which God in Christ Jesus is calling
us upward.

Philippians 3:13,14

God is not concerned about whether we
reach perfection but whether we are pressing
toward the mark of perfection. Speak and act
with the knowledge that Jesus is alive and
working in your life, and no matter how big
a mistake you make, Jesus' shed blood
covers it.

2

⊸⇆⊷

Celebrate the Positive

The second key to overcoming insecurity is related to the first: *Meditate on and speak positive things about yourself.*

We have learned how destructive thinking and saying negative things about ourselves can be. Now let's look at the power of thinking and saying positive things about ourselves that line up with the Word.

As we have seen, our thoughts and words about ourselves are tremendously important. We need to meditate on good things about ourselves — on purpose. We need to look for good things about ourselves, think on those things and speak them to ourselves.

If we talk about ourselves in a negative way, we begin to see ourselves in a negative way. Soon we begin to convey that negativism to all those around us. It is literally true that others' opinions of us will never rise above the opinion we have of ourselves.

If I am around people who are confident and convey that confidence, I find I automatically have confidence in them. But if they convey to me that they don't believe in themselves, I find it very hard to have confidence in them.

That same principle applies to us. If we want others to have confidence in us, we must show them we have confidence in ourselves.

Giants or Grasshoppers?

> There we saw the Nephilim [or giants], the sons of Anak, who come from the giants; and we were in our own sight as grasshoppers, and so we were in their sight.

> *Numbers 13:33*

In the book of Numbers there is an account of twelve spies sent out into the

Promised Land to scout out the land. Ten came back with an evil report, and two came back with a good report. The ten who came back with the evil report saw giants in the land and were frightened: "We were in our own sight as grasshoppers, and so we were in their sight." In other words, the enemy saw them the same way they saw themselves.

These ten spies ran home defeated. Why? Because they did not have the ability to over-come the giants in the land? No. They ran home defeated because of the way they saw themselves, because of the negative attitude they had toward themselves.

The Power of Positive Confession

Caleb quieted the people before Moses, and said, Let us go up at once and possess it; we are well able to conquer it.

Numbers 13:30

Here we see the response of one of the two positive spies, Caleb. In the face of seemingly overwhelming odds, his report was, "We are well able." The reason he said that was because he knew that God had told them to go into and take possession of the land.

In order to overcome the negative thinking and speaking that have been such a natural part of our lifestyle for so long, we must make a conscious effort to think and speak good things about ourselves to ourselves by making positive confessions.

Perhaps you think you would rather not go around talking to yourself, but you do. Even if you don't talk out loud, you have what is called "self-talk" going on inside you all the time.

I encourage you to begin speaking positively in private, for example when you are taking a shower or driving in the car alone. Begin to speak, on purpose, good things about yourself.

Confess in Line With the Word of God

> ...But we have the mind of Christ
> (the Messiah) and do hold the
> thoughts (feelings and purposes) of
> His heart.

> *1 Corinthians 2:16*

When I say that we should make positive confession about ourselves, I mean that we need to get our mouth in line with what the Word says about us. For example, the Word of God says we have the mind of Christ. So that is what we should be saying about ourselves.

The Bible also says we have a call on our life, that every one of us is called into the ministry of reconciliation and intercession. (2 Corinthians 5:18-20; 1 Timothy 2:1-3.) That does not mean that we all stand in the office of an intercessor, but we all have the call on our life to be used by God — and we should say so.

Speak Scriptural Confessions

> ...speak and publish fearlessly the
> Word of God....
>
> *Philippians 1:14*

Many years ago God put in my heart to make a list of confessions about my life. By the time I was done there were over a hundred.

I found Scriptures to back up each confession I put on my list. It took me time to do that. But if you will make an effort to dig around in the Word for yourself, you will find gold in there.

When I began speaking these confessions, the things I started saying were not happening. They were not reality in my life at that moment.

For example, at that time I was living under a cloud of guilt and condemnation. But several times every day I would say, "I am the righteousness of God in Jesus Christ. I have been set apart and made holy by the

Lamb. There is a call on my life, and God is going to use me."

I had such a bad attitude about myself, I had to convince myself I was okay before God could really do anything through me.

For six months, I was diligent to read that list at least once or twice every day. I still remember a good portion of those positive confessions. Those words are now built into me.

Believe in Yourself — In What God Can Do Through You

> ...We are not able to go up against
> the people [of Canaan], for they are
> stronger than we are.
>
> *Numbers 13:31*

God needs you. But if you don't believe in yourself, if you don't believe in the ability God has placed on the inside of you, you will discount yourself. You will sit on the sidelines and watch other people be used by God in your place.

God deliberately chooses the weak and foolish things of the world to do His work to confound the wise, so that no mortal can ever have reason to glory or to boast in his own flesh. (1 Corinthians 1:27-29.)

God is not as concerned with your weaknesses as you are. The problem with the spies in Numbers 13 is they looked at the giants instead of looking at God. Yes, there were giants in the land, but the Israelites needed to look at God and not the giants.

There are some giants in my life. But I don't need to stare at those giants. I need to stare at God. I need to keep my gaze firmly fixed on God and believe that He can do what He says He can.

The same is true for you. Your spirit wants to produce tremendous things in your life. But if you always keep that spirit man pushed down by negative attitudes, thoughts

and words, he will never rise up to bring you
into the place God wants you to occupy, into
the land He wants you to possess.

God Gives Life to the Dead

As it is written, I have made you
the father of many nations. [He was
appointed our father] in the sight of
God in Whom he believed, Who
gives life to the dead and speaks of
the nonexistent things that [He has
foretold and promised] as if they
[already] existed.

Romans 4:17

Abraham knew it was not a sin to do or
be something if it was in line with the Word
of God.

Before Abraham ever had a child God told
him that he was to be the father of many
nations. Yet how could that be? Abraham was
an old man, and his wife Sarah was barren.

But God "gives life to the dead." He proved that by quickening Sarah's dead womb and sparking up Abraham's dead body. And God "speaks of the nonexistent things that [He has foretold and promised] as if they [already] existed."

Based upon this Scripture we should get our mouths in line with anything that God has promised in the Word. That does not mean that we are to go around speaking any off-the-wall thing we want to. We must speak only those things promised us in the Word of God.

Confessing the Word Brings Results

So shall you find favor, good understanding, and high esteem in the sight
[or judgment] of God and man.

Proverbs 3:4

I used to have major problems in my life. Now I am walking in victory because the Word of God has worked in my life. But I did not just fall out of bed one morning and begin to experience immediate and total victory. Nor did I just drop into a meeting once every three weeks and listen to a tape occasionally. I have had my nose in the Word ever since I became baptized in the Holy Spirit. I began to experience victory by continually exalting the Word of God in my life.

I expect favor because I have quoted Scriptures on favor to myself for a long time. The Bible says repeatedly that we have favor with God and that God will give us favor with man. I expect to get favor with men. That is not a bad, prideful attitude; it is not improper. Why? Because it is a promise to me in the Bible.

If you will speak about yourself what the Word of God says about you, you will receive positive results, but it will take time and effort.

When God first started teaching me these things I am sharing with you in this book I had a weight problem. I had always been about twenty to twenty-five pounds overweight. I remember standing in front of a full-length mirror looking at myself and saying, "I eat right, I look good, I feel good and I weigh 135 pounds."

At that time, *none* of that was true. I did not eat right, I did not look good, I did not feel good and I *certainly* did not weigh 135 pounds. But I felt that was a good weight for me, so I began confessing it to myself.

I did not go tapping other people on the shoulder saying, "Hey! I look good, I feel good, I eat right and I weigh 135 pounds." These were private confessions about myself that I made to myself.

So Goes the Mouth, So Goes the Life

For we all often stumble and fall and offend in many things. And if anyone does not offend in speech [never says the wrong things], he is a

fully developed character and a
perfect man, able to control his whole
body and to curb his entire nature.

James 3:2

Positive confession of the Word of God
should be an ingrained habit of every believer.

If you have not yet begun to develop this
important habit, start today. Begin thinking and
saying good things about yourself: "I am the
righteousness of God in Jesus Christ. I prosper
in everything I lay my hand to. I have gifts and
talents, and God is using me. I operate in the
fruit of the Spirit. I walk in love. Joy flows
through me. I eat right, I look good, I feel good,
I weigh exactly what I should weigh."

Even though God wants to help us, the
Bible teaches we get our lives straightened
out by getting our mouth straightened out. It
teaches we can appropriate the blessings of
God in our lives by believing and confessing
the positive things God has said about us in
His Word.

3

~

Avoid Comparisons

The next step to overcoming insecurity is simple: *Never compare yourself with anyone else.*

If you lack confidence, this is an important point. You may think you are perfectly all right until you look around and see somebody else who seems to be doing what you are doing a little better than you are.

Take prayer as an example. Many times even personal communion with God can be a source of condemnation. Compared to someone else you may feel you are not praying long enough, good enough or "spiritually" enough.

Comparison Invites Condemnation

Do you have faith? Have it to yourself before God. Happy is he

who does not condemn himself in
what he approves.

Romans 14:22 NKJV

There was a time in my life when I was
praying about half an hour a day. I was just
as happy as I could be doing that because
there was an anointing on me to pray thirty
minutes each day. I was perfectly content
and satisfied with my daily half-hour fellow-
ship with the Lord.

Then one day I heard a minister preach
about how he prayed four hours every day
and got up at some awful hour to do it. (At
least it seemed awful to me — I think he
started at four or five o'clock in the morning.)
When I compared myself to him, I felt like a
wretch even though I had been honestly and
truly happy about my prayer life up to that
point. After hearing that message I felt as
though I hardly even loved God.

Sometimes I would hear people preach
about how God would get them up in the

middle of the night to pray. I would think, "Lord, what's the matter with me? I go to bed and sleep!"

Why was I put under condemnation? Because I really was not secure in who I was in Christ.

As a minister I have learned to be careful about what I say because many of those to whom I preach are not secure. There is a danger they will take my testimony and compare themselves to me. So for the most part I keep to myself how long I pray and how I pray and what I pray about.

We Are All Unique

For he who serves Christ in these things is acceptable to God and approved by men.

Romans 14:18 NKJV

We can feel perfectly fine about ourselves until we start comparing ourselves with somebody else. Then all of a sudden, we think we are an awful mess.

I really want to encourage you to stop comparing yourself with other people: how you look compared to how they look, what position you occupy compared to what position they occupy, how long you pray compared to how long they pray, how often you prophesy compared to how often they prophesy.

Likewise, you cannot compare your tribulation to someone else's tribulation. You cannot compare your suffering to someone else's suffering. Some situations may seem hard to you. But you cannot look at somebody else and say, "Why is all this happening to me and everything comes up roses for you?"

For example, perhaps two young women in the same neighborhood get born again. Ten years down the road both are still believing for their husbands' salvation but neither has been saved. Then a woman across the street gets born again. She believes God for her husband to get saved and two weeks later, he is born again, filled with the Spirit and ready to start running around the world preaching.

God Knows What He Is Doing

> For I know the thoughts and plans that I have for you, says the Lord, thoughts and plans for welfare and peace and not for evil, to give you hope in your final outcome.
>
> *Jeremiah 29:11*

If you don't understand that God has an individual plan for your life, you will begin to look around and compare yourself with other people and say, "What's wrong with me? I have been praying ten years and haven't gotten an answer; you've been praying two weeks and look what God has done for you."

People tell me all the time how they work in the church, tithe, love God and are trying as hard as they know how. Yet it seems as though nothing ever works out for them while others around them seem to get everything they desire. Why is that?

I don't have a pat answer to that question, but I do know this: We have to believe above everything else that God knows what He is doing. It is amazing the peace that comes with that belief.

Walking By Faith, Not Sight

For we walk by faith...not by sight
or appearance.

2 Corinthians 5:7

Sometimes when people have a call on their life, they go through things that others may never go through.

Because of the things I went through for a period of four or five years in particular, I have deep, heart-felt understanding and compassion for hurting people when they come to me for ministry. There are some things that cannot be received by the laying on of hands. They come only through personal experience.

The experience I had helped prepare me for my ministry.

In the beginning of my ministry I would cry out, "Why, God, why? I'm believing You. I don't understand why this is happening to me."

Many times we do not understand something until we get on the other side of it, when it is all over and we are rejoicing in victory. Perhaps a year or more after the experience is over, our eyes are opened and we are able to say, "Now I understand."

Or we may never understand. But when we learn to trust God even if we don't understand, our faith will grow.

Don't Compare, Just Follow!

He said this to indicate by what kind of death Peter would glorify God. And after this, He said to him, Follow Me!

But Peter turned and saw the disciple whom Jesus loved, following

— the one who also had leaned back on His breast at the supper and had said, Lord, who is it that is going to betray You?

When Peter saw him, he said to Jesus, Lord, what about this man?

John 21:19-21

Just as we must guard against comparing our gifts and talents with the gifts and talents of others, so we must not compare our trials and tribulations with their trials and tribulations.

Jesus revealed to Peter ahead of time some of the suffering he would go through. Peter immediately wanted to compare his suffering and his lot in life with somebody else's by saying, "What about this man?"

"Jesus said to him, If I want him to stay (survive, live) till I come, what is that to you? [What concern is it of yours?] You follow Me!" (John 21:22).

That is His answer to us also. We are not called to compare, only to comply.

Don't Covet the Blessings of Others

You shall not covet....

Exodus 20:17

When you are having a hard time, never look at others and say, "God, I don't understand. Why am I having such a hard time while they just seem to be so blessed?" That kind of question only brings torment. Why? Because it is a sign of covetousness.

When your brothers or sisters are blessed, be joyful for them; when they hurt, share their pain with them. (Romans 12:15.) But don't compare yourself to others. Instead trust God. Believe that He has an individualized, specialized plan for your life. Be secure in the knowledge that no matter what is happening to you or how things may appear for the moment, He cares about you very much and is working out everything for the best. (1 Peter 5:7; Romans 8:28.)

4

⮑

Focus on Potential, Not Limitations

This is the fourth point in how to succeed at being yourself, how to build confidence and overcome insecurity: *Focus on potential instead of limitations.* In other words, focus on your strengths instead of your weaknesses.

Concentrate on Potential

> Having gifts (faculties, talents, qualities) that differ according to the grace given us, let us use them....
>
> *Romans 12:6*

The well-known actress Helen Hayes was only five feet tall. In the early days of her career, she was told that if she were just four inches taller, she could be a great stage star. Although she could not actually grow to increase her height, she worked to improve her posture and bearing, to stand tall, so that on stage she appeared taller.[1]

Instead of concentrating on the fact that she was only five feet tall, she began concentrating on her great acting potential, and she didn't give up. Later on in her life, she was chosen to portray Mary, Queen of Scots, one of the tallest queens who has ever lived.[2]

Focus on your potential instead of on your limitations.

You Can Do What God Has Called You To Do

> ...I can do everything God asks me
> to with the help of Christ who gives
> me the strength and power.
>
> *Philippians 4:13 TLB*

Recently I saw a sign on a church that said, "Trust in God, believe in yourself and you can do anything." That is not correct.

There was a time in my life when I would have seen that sign and said, "Amen!" But not anymore. You and I really cannot do *anything* we want to do. We cannot do anything or everything that everyone else is doing. But we can do everything *God has called us to do.* And we can be anything *God says we can be.*

We must get balance in this area. We can go to motivational seminars and be told with a lot of emotional hype, "You can do anything. Think you can do it; believe you can do it; say you can do it — and you can do it!" That is true only to a degree. Carried too far, it gets off into humanism. We need to speak about ourselves what the *Word* says about us.

We can do what we are *called* to do, what we are gifted to do. There are ways we can learn to recognize the grace gifts that are on our life.

I have learned this regarding myself: When I start getting frustrated, I know it is a sign that either I have gotten off into my own works and am no longer receiving God's grace, or I am trying to do something for which there was no grace to begin with.

Don't Frustrate the Grace of God

I do not frustrate the grace of God....

Galatians 2:21 KJV

God has not called us to frustration.

Each of us is full of gifts and talents and potentials and abilities. If we really begin to cooperate with God, we can go for the very best that God has for us. But if we get high-minded ideas and set goals that are beyond our abilities and the grace gifts on our life, we will become frustrated. We will not attain those things, and we may even end up blaming God for our failure.

Strength For All Things in Christ

I have strength for all things in Christ Who empowers me [I am ready for anything and equal to any-thing through Him Who infuses inner strength into me; I am self-suf-ficient in Christ's sufficiency].

Philippians 4:13

If we just pull that Scripture out of the Bible, it certainly looks like we ought to be able to do anything we want to do, doesn't it?

If we pick out the verses we want, we can make the Bible say anything we want it to say. But let's read this passage in context and see what it really says. Let's begin at verse 10:

> I was made very happy in the Lord that now you have revived your interest in my welfare after so long a time; you were indeed thinking of me, but you had no opportunity to show it.

The people in the Philippian Church had sent Paul an offering, which pleased him. He was writing to say, "Friends, I am happy you have revived your interest in me after such a long time." Then he went on to add in verses 11 and 12:

> Not that I am implying that I was in any personal want, for I have learned how to be content (satisfied to the point where I am not disturbed or disquieted) in whatever state I am.

I know how to be abased and live
humbly in straitened circumstances...

(That means there were times when Paul
did *not* have everything he wanted, times
when his circumstances were *not* the way he
would have liked them to be.)

...and I know also how to enjoy
plenty and live in abundance. I have
learned in any and all circumstances the secret of facing every
situation, whether well-fed or going
hungry, having a sufficiency and
enough to spare or going without
and being in want.

Paul's message was not that he could do
anything he set his mind to, but that he had
learned the secret of making the best of whatever situation he found himself in. It is in that
context that he makes the statement we hear
quoted so often about the ability to "do all
things in Christ."

The Truth About "Doing All Things"

I have strength for all things in Christ Who empowers me [I am ready for anything and equal to anything through Him Who infuses inner strength into me; I am self-sufficient in Christ's sufficiency].

Philippians 4:13

When we read verse 13 in context, we realize what Paul is actually saying: "God has done a work in my life. I have learned the secret of staying at peace whether I have everything I want or not. If my circumstances are exciting, I know how to handle that situation and stay humble. If my circumstances aren't too good, I have the inner strength to deal with that situation, also. I am able to handle all the varying situations of life through Christ Who gives me strength."

If Philippians 4:13 is taken out of its context, we might believe we can do anything we feel like, anytime we want to, anywhere we want to. That is not true. We must stay with the anointing, which only comes with the will of God.

Stay With the Anointing

But it is God Who confirms and makes us steadfast and establishes us [in joint fellowship]...in Christ, and has consecrated and anointed us [enduing us with the gifts of the Holy Spirit].

2 Corinthians 1:21

You may have experienced deep confusion at some time in your life by trying to do something for which God has not consecrated and anointed you. You thought it was God's will, then discovered it was not. If so, you are not the only one who has done this. I have done the same thing and so have many others. But then how can you ever know that something is truly of God?

If you believe God has spoken something to you — it has a scriptural basis, and you really have peace about it — then move toward it. But if you discover that no matter what you do, nothing works, don't spend your life banging your head against a brick wall trying to force something that God is not helping you with. If there is no anointing, it will never work.

Some people spend all their lives trying to ride a dead horse. I heard someone say recently, "The horse has been dead seven years — it's time to dismount."

Do your part. Do what you believe is right, follow God's leadership to the best of your ability, then leave the outcome in His hands. In this way you are doing all that you can, but you are not spending your life trying to do what you can't do, which is God's part.

Leave It in God's Hands

...and having done all,...stand.

Ephesians 6:13 KJV

Remember, if God has called you to do something, do your part and then stand firm.

When you have done all you can do, leave the situation in God's hands and go on about your business. If He does not do His part, then it is not time, it is not right or it is not for you.

People often ask me, "How can I do what you're doing? God has called me to preach like you. Tell me how you got started." I tell them, "It's not that easy. I can't just give you three easy lessons on how to begin a ministry. But if God calls you, He opens the doors. He apprehends you, prepares you, provides the money, gives you favor and makes it happen."

It is okay to confess that you are going to have a ministry similar to another person's if you believe God has called you to do so. Just be sure to make that confession in the privacy of your home, not in public. Keep it mainly between you and God until God makes it public. If that desire is of God, you will see it come to pass. But if it is not of

God and nothing happens, that still should not affect your sense of self-worth.

You have to believe in yourself. It is okay to look at somebody who is successful in ministry or in business and say, "I believe if God wants me in that position, He will make me able to do it. I have potential, and I have ability." Just make sure that it is God's will for you and not your own selfish desire. If it is God's will, you will find joy in it.

Do What You Love, Love What You Do!

If God has called you to do something, you will find yourself loving it despite any adversity that may beset you.

Sometimes Dave and I have to leave some place at three o'clock in the morning with only three hours of sleep. Often I have had to sleep in the back of the van — that's like trying to sleep while riding a horse. Some of the bathrooms we have to use when on the road are not very nice. Some of the restaurants we eat in are not very good.

Some of our hotel accommodations are awful, and I wake up in the morning feeling like I am about a hundred years old. Sometimes I have to study on the bed in a motel because there is no desk.

Like Paul, my husband and I face undesirable conditions again and again. But I love what I am doing. How could I love it if it was not of God? In spite of all the hardships and inconveniences, we truly enjoy traveling all over the country doing the work of the Lord.

If God has called you to do something, He enables you to do it. If you are struggling all the time saying, "I hate this," something is wrong!

God Gives Promotion

> For not from the east nor from the west nor from the south come promotion and lifting up.
>
> But God is the Judge! He puts down one and lifts up another.
>
> *Psalm 75:6,7*

Often we humans ask other people, "What's your occupation?" When they answer, sometimes we imply by our attitude that they should have a desire for a higher position than the one they presently occupy.

It is okay to believe God for a greater position or responsibility, but it is equally acceptable to remain in the position we are in if that is where we feel God wants us.

God can enable us to fill a position and do a job that, in the natural world, we are not qualified for. But there are some insecure people who think they can gain worth and value through a higher position. They step out on their own without God's leading, their motive is wrong and they fall flat on their face.

I have discovered that it is unwise to try to get a position that God is not giving to us. We can labor in the flesh and make things happen, but we will never be at peace with the results.

Therefore humble yourselves [demote, lower yourselves in your

own estimation] under the mighty
hand of God, that in due time He
may exalt you.

1 Peter 5:6

God does things in our lives when He
knows we are truly ready. Set high goals, but
let your focus be on doing the very best you
can where you are, knowing that if and when
God wants to promote you, He is certainly
well able to do so.

Focus on Potential

All these [gifts, achievements, abil-
ities] are inspired and brought to pass
by one and the same [Holy] Spirit,
Who apportions to each person indi-
vidually [exactly] as He chooses.

1 Corinthians 12:11

Gifts and talents are distributed by the
Holy Spirit according to the grace that is on
each person to handle them. God is not dis-
pleased with us if we have only one gift

while somebody else has five gifts. But He does not like it if we do not develop the one gift we do have. (Matthew 25:14-30.)

In the book of Numbers we saw that twelve spies were sent in to scout out the Promised Land they had been commanded by God to possess. Ten of them came back saying, "There are giants in the land, so we can't take it." But two of them said, "Yes, there are giants there, but we are well able to take it because *God* has said to do so."

Ten of the Hebrew spies looked at their limitations; two looked at their potential. Ten of them looked at the giants; two looked at God.

If you are going to like yourself, if you are going to succeed at being yourself, you are going to have to focus on your potential — what God has created you to be — not on your limitations.

5

~

Exercise Your Gift

Here is the fifth point in overcoming insecurity: *Find something you like to do and that you do well, then do it over and over.* Do you know what will happen? You will begin to succeed because you will be doing what you are gifted to do. And you will start to feel better about yourself because you won't be constantly failing.

Locate Your Gift

[He whose gift is] practical service, let him give himself to serving; he who teaches, to his teaching.

Romans 12:7

That Scripture does not say, "If you are a teacher, teach, but at the same time try real hard to be a worship leader."

There was a time in my life when I was really mad at myself because all I could do was teach. I wanted to do all the other things I saw everybody else doing. I struggled and prayed and "tore down strongholds." I told the devil, "I'm going to do more!" But I came to a place where I had to be satisfied preaching the Word.

I spent a year of my life trying to grow tomatoes and make my husband's clothes because my next door neighbor did that. I compared myself with her and concluded there was something wrong with me because I didn't act like a "normal" housewife. Frankly, I did not want to grow tomatoes. And I *really* didn't want to make my husband's clothes. But I got all hung up in trying to do what others were doing.

Don't Keep Doing What You Don't Do Well

Except the Lord builds the house,
they labor in vain who build it....

Psalm 127:1

I spent a year trying to do something that I did not do well. Day in and day out I had continual defeat. I was so discouraged. I might spend all day sewing on a shirt, then hem it on the wrong side and have to spend hours picking the hem out. I continually felt defeated.

Don't spend all your time trying to do something you are not good at. Instead, let God show you what you are good at. Generally, the things you are good at are the things you are going to enjoy.

God wouldn't make us do something we hated all of our life. Why are we always trying to do something we can't do? Why not just find something we do well and go for it? It is amazing how much better it makes us feel.

Look for the Anointing

But as for you, the anointing (the sacred appointment, the unction) which you received from Him abides [permanently] in you; [so] then you have no need that anyone should instruct you....

1 John 2:27

A lot of people in ministry try to do things they are not anointed to do just because other people do them.

In my travels, I see ministers all over the country who are struggling. Often the reason is that they are trying to do what some other church or ministry is doing even though God has not anointed them to do it. They feel if they cannot do what someone else is doing, they are not as good as that person.

We can only do what God has gifted us and anointed us to do. If we try to do otherwise, we will feel pressured continually.

Don't Exceed God's Grace

John answered, A man can receive nothing [he can claim nothing, he can take unto himself nothing] except as it has been granted to him from heaven. [A man must be content to receive the gift which is given him from heaven; there is no other source.]

John 3:27

A man can receive how much? A man can claim how much? He can take unto himself how much? Only as much as is granted to him from heaven.

As Christians we must be *content.* If I can never preach as well as some other preacher, I am just going to have to be content to preach the best I can. If my ministry never gets as big as Brother So-and-So's or Sister So-and-So's, I must be content with what I have.

You and I cannot go beyond the grace of God in our life. We cannot receive a gift from God just because we want one. The Holy Spirit gives us gifts according to His will for us, and we must be satisfied with what we receive from Him.

Sometimes even though God wants to confer a gift upon us, it is not yet time for it to be bestowed. Until God leans over the bannister of heaven and says, "Now!" we can struggle and fume and fuss and fight and complain and quarrel, but we will still not get it.

Do you know when we are going to get what God wants us to have? When He gets ready to give it to us. We are not going to get it until then, so we may as well learn to be content with such things as we have. (Hebrews 13:5 KJV.) We must remember that "Father knows best"!

Use Your Gift

Having gifts (faculties, talents, qualities) that differ according to the grace given us, let us use them: [He whose gift is] prophecy, [let him prophesy] according to the proportion of his faith;

[He whose gift is] practical service, let him give himself to serving; he who teaches, to his teaching;

He who exhorts (encourages), to his exhortation; he who contributes, let him do it in simplicity and liberality....

Romans 12:6-8

Don't waste time trying to figure out what your gift is. Just start functioning in what you are good at.

I remember a woman who led worship in a church we visited in Maine. She was an exhorter. When I had finished preaching she chased me down the back stairs, "Oh, come here, come here," she said, and began praying for me.

Then she began speaking to me. "Oh, honey, that was wonderful, that was marvelous. Oh, you're so anointed."

She just carried on! By the time I left I felt *great,* like I was floating on air!

Sometimes I work really hard and feel that I have fallen flat. Then here come the exhorters in the church. The more they say to me, the more I believe I am able to start all over again.

But what does the devil say to an exhorter? "That's nothing, just being able to cheer people up." He is not about to tell that person that exhortation is an important ministry in the church.

If you have the gift of exhortation, Satan will tell you that you ought to preach or teach or become a pastor or build a church! But the Bible says if your gift is exhorting, then begin to exhort. If you are to teach, then begin teaching. If you are to give yourself in serving, then start serving. If you are to help others, then start helping.

The Ministry of Helps

...he who gives aid and superintends,
with zeal and singleness of mind....

Romans 12:8

If you are to give aid in the Body of Christ, then make it your business to give. If God calls you to be a giver, He is obviously going to provide you the means to do that.

The phrase "he who gives aid" refers to the helpers. There are many people in the Body of Christ who are called as servants, as helpers, as those whose job it is to assist a ministry.

God calls strong leaders, people upon whom He bestows a powerful anointing for leadership. It is a gift to lead large numbers of people while keeping things in proper order. If an individual does not have the gift to do that, he will soon get himself into big trouble.

But even if he is gifted for the position, the leader can't do everything, so God anoints other people to help him, to hold up his hands, to pray for him. No one can exercise any kind of successful ministry without those who have been called and anointed to help.

If that is your calling and anointing, do it with all your might because it is vitally important.

Some people say, "Well, I'm just in helps." No, they are not *just* in helps. They are in one of the greatest ministries in the Bible. There are more people in helps than in any other ministry of the Church.

If you believe you are called into the ministry of serving, I hope you will never again feel insulted because "all you are is in helps." After all, that is the ministry of the Holy Spirit.

The Holy Spirit Is the Helper

And I will ask the Father, and He will give you another Comforter (Counselor, Helper, Intercessor, Advocate, Strengthener, and Standby), that He may remain with you forever.

John 14:16

The helps ministry is a great, marvelous, wonderful, powerful ministry. The Holy

Spirit is in the ministry of helps. He leads it. He is *the* Helper. He is the One Who walks alongside each believer waiting to provide whatever assistance may be needed.

Some people are insulted because they have been called into the ministry of helps. They struggle with themselves trying to be something else. They simply do not realize that they exercise the same ministry the Holy Spirit exercises.

Be a Blessing Where You Are

...he who does acts of mercy, with genuine cheerfulness and joyful eagerness.

Romans 12:8

There are certain things you and I like to do as a result of our gifts from God. We may not think those things are important — but they are, as we will discover if we will just begin to do them.

You can be a blessing to people no matter how simple your gifts may be. If you are a good cook or love to bake, use your gifts and talents to bless somebody other than yourself.

One night a friend brought my husband and me a pot of soup. It was the best soup I had ever tasted in my whole life; I just loved it. We talked for days about how wonderful the soup was.

Later our friend told us she kept thinking as she was making the soup, "I need to take Joyce some of this." But she dismissed the idea thinking it was silly. "She's not going to want my soup."

How many times does the devil cheat us out of being a blessing? Do you know the greatest thing you can do is be a blessing? Stop trying to figure out what your gift is and begin to function in something you like to do — just get busy and do it.

If you like to cheer people up, make it your business to cheer them up. If you love to give, find something and give it away. If you love to help, then help everybody you can. Just bless people.

We don't always have to do some *great* spiritual thing. Actually some of the things we don't think are really spiritual are more important to God than the things we think are so great.

Stir Up Your Gift

Wherefore I put thee in remembrance that thou stir up the gift of God, which is in thee....

2 Timothy 1:6 KJV

So many times we look for some great "spiritual" experience. We go to bed at night and the devil says, "Well, you didn't do a thing worthwhile today." But if we touched somebody else's life, if we made someone else happy, if we put a smile on someone's face, we *did* do something worthwhile. That ability is a gift from God.

The great apostle Paul tells his young disciple Timothy to stir up the gifts within him. That is good advice for all of us. Sometimes we get lazy with our gifts. We need to stir up those gifts on purpose. We need to "get with the program" again.

If you want to overcome a sense of worthlessness and insecurity, stir up your gift. Start using what God has put in you. Get busy and do what you can with what you have.

Do what you like to do. Then do it over and over.

6

~

Have the Courage To Be Different

If you are going to overcome insecurity and be the person you are called to be in Christ, *you must have the courage to be different.*

Even though each of us *is* different, we still try to be like each other. That is what causes unhappiness.

Don't Be Like Everyone Else

Now am I trying to win the favor of men, or of God? Do I seek to please men? If I were still seeking popularity with men, I should not be a bond servant of Christ (the Messiah).

Galatians 1:10

If you are going to be a success at being completely and fully you, you are going to have to take a chance on not being like everyone else.

Why not ask yourself the question Paul asked? Are you trying to win the favor of men, or of God?

Menpleasers or Godpleasers?

> Not with eyeservice, as men-pleasers; but as the servants of Christ, doing the will of God from the heart.
>
> *Ephesians 6:6 KJV*

Becoming menpleasers is one of the easiest things we can do but one that can ultimately make us very unhappy. When we begin pleasing other people we begin to hear comments that make us feel good about ourselves. That is okay as long as we do not derive our sense of worth from it. As believers, our sense of worth has to be rooted and grounded not in the opinions of men but in the love of God.

We are worth something because God sent His only Son to die for us. We are worth something because God loves us, not because of what everybody else thinks about us or says about us.

We become "menpleasers" when we no longer do the things we want to do, but what everybody else wants us to do because we think that will gain us acceptance and approval.

That was not the attitude the apostle Paul had or advocated.

Don't Let Others Manipulate You

Moreover, it is [essentially] required of stewards that a man should be found faithful [proving himself worthy of trust].

But [as for me personally] it matters very little to me that I should be put on trial by you [on this point], and that you or any other human tribunal should investigate and question and cross-question me. I do not even put myself on trial and judge myself.

1 Corinthians 4:2,3

That is a very liberating attitude — not to be concerned with public opinion or even self-opinion.

How far do you think Jesus would have gotten if He had worried about what people thought? Philippians 2:7 KJV says Jesus purposely "made himself of no reputation." As I was pondering that verse one day, Jesus said, "I got that over with right away." Eventually so did I. Now I no longer feel I have to run around trying to please people all the time.

I must admit I don't like it when people are unhappy with me. I don't even like it if one of my own children gets upset with me. But I know I cannot let people manipulate me with their demands.

As followers of Christ, we are to be led by the Spirit, not controlled by people. In the same manner, we should not try to control others, but allow them to be led by the Spirit just as we are.

Walk in Love

And walk in love...as Christ loved
us and gave Himself up for us....

Ephesians 5:2

The point is, if we know we are doing the
best we know how, we should not let other
people's opinions of us bother us.

Still we must walk in love. We cannot just
do anything we want to, anytime we want to.
We cannot say, "Whoever doesn't like it,
that's tough, that's their problem." Love does
not behave that way.

Yet we must not allow people to manipulate and control us to the point we are never
free to be who we are. If we do, we will
always be trying to become whatever we
think others expect us to be.

Be Transformed, Not Conformed

Do not be conformed to this world
(this age), [fashioned after and ad-
apted to its external, superficial cus-
toms], but be transformed (changed)

by the [entire] renewal of your mind
[by its new ideals and its new atti-
tude], so that you may prove [for
yourselves] what is the good and
acceptable and perfect will of God,
even the thing which is good and
acceptable and perfect [in His sight
for you].

Romans 12:2

The world is continually trying to conform
us to its image. When I say "the world," I
mean those we know and deal with on a daily
basis. It may be family, friends, people in the
neighborhood or even the church.

The word *conform* means "1. To be similar
in form or character. 2....COMPLY. 3. To
behave in accordance with prevailing modes
or customs."[1]

People will always try to get us to fit into
their mold, partly due to their own insecurity.
It makes them feel better about what they are
doing if they can get someone else to do it too.

Very few people have the ability just to be who they are and let everybody else be who they are. Can you imagine how nice the world would be if we would all do that? Each person could be secure in who he is and would let others be who they are. We would not have to try to be little clones of one another.

Be Different — Become an Innovator

> Behold, I am doing a new thing! Now it springs forth; do you not perceive and know it and will you not give heed to it?....

> *Isaiah 43:19*

All the great reformers in the Church, like Martin Luther, and in the world have been people who stepped out of the mold and did things differently. The same is true of the great men and women in the Bible.

Jeremiah was very young to be called as a prophet of God. The excuse he gave God was, "I'm too young."

Timothy also said, "I'm too young." Paul had to encourage Timothy over and over: "Don't worry about your youth, Timothy. God has called you and anointed you. Keep your eyes on that call."

What if John the Baptist or the apostle Paul or even Jesus had not had the courage to be different? We look at the great men and women in the Bible and think how wonderful they were. But they paid a price. They had to step out and be innovators. They had to be different. They had to avoid being ruled and controlled by what everybody thought they should be.

Operate in the Fruit of the Spirit

But the fruit of the [Holy] Spirit [the work which His presence within accomplishes] is love, joy (gladness), peace, patience (an even temper, forbearance), kindness, goodness (benevolence), faithfulness,

Gentleness (meekness, humility), self-control (self-restraint, continence). Against such things there is no law [that can bring a charge].

Galatians 5:22,23

Even if we decide we are going to be innovative and different, we still need to operate in the fruit of the Spirit. We must not go around with a sarcastic, rebellious attitude. At the same time we cannot live our lives being conformed to the world because God wants to use us. He has something He wants to do through us.

God Wants To Use Us

While they were worshiping the Lord and fasting, the Holy Spirit said, Separate now for Me Barnabas and Saul for the work to which I have called them.

Acts 13:2

God wants to take us with all our weaknesses and inabilities and transform us, by working from the inside out, to do something powerful in this earth.

Satan will use the world and the world system to try to keep us out of God's will, out of God's best for us. Satan will try to get us to conform to what the world wants by telling us if we don't, we will be rejected.

If we are going to stand up and overcome insecurity, if we are going to succeed at being ourselves, we cannot continue to be afraid of what everybody else may think.

If we are seeking to be popular, there is a real good chance we are going to miss the will of God for our life.

Say Yes to the Call of God

Also I heard the voice of the Lord, saying, Whom shall I send? And who will go for Us? Then said I, Here am I; send me.

Isaiah 6:8

I would be miserable right now if I had said no to the call of God on my life. I might have stayed home and tried to grow tomatoes and sew my husband's clothes because that's what I thought would cause me to fit into the neighborhood. But I would have been miserable all of my life. Get hold of this truth today for your own life.

When God began showing Dave and me teachings about healing and the baptism of the Spirit and the gifts of the Spirit, we were going to a church where such ideas and practices were not popular or even acceptable. We ended up having to leave that church and all of our friends.

We were involved in everything in that church. Our whole life revolved around it. But we were told, "If you are going to believe the things you say you believe, then we can no longer have anything to do with you." What those people were really saying was, "Joyce, look, we've got a system here,

and what you and Dave are doing doesn't fit
into it. If you want to stay here, you must
forget that stuff and fit into our mold."

The decision to leave that church was a
difficult one. But if I had conformed to their
demands, I would have missed the will of
God for my life.

You Will Come Out Victorious

Jesus said, Truly I tell you, there is
no one who has given up and left
house or brothers or sisters or mother
or father or children or lands for My
sake and for the Gospel's

Who will not receive a hundred
times as much now in this time —
houses and brothers and sisters and
mothers and children and lands,
with persecutions — and in the age
to come, eternal life.

Mark 10:29,30

After we left that church, I went through times of intense loneliness. But now I have more friends than I had before.

If God calls you to step out, the world will demand that you conform. Decide for God. You will go through trials — that's part of the challenge. You will go through a period of loneliness. There will be other problems. But you will come out on the other side victorious. You will be able to lie down at night and have that peace inside knowing that, even if you may not be popular with everybody else, you are pleasing to God.

Please God, Not Men

...You are My Son, My Beloved!
In You I am well pleased and find delight!

Luke 3:22

Jesus must have felt good when that voice came out of heaven at His baptism saying, "This is my beloved Son, in whom I

am well pleased..." (Matthew 17:5 KJV). But
until that time in His life, there were few
people who understood Him or liked what
He was doing.

As we have seen, Paul refused to be
judged by others or by himself. If he had
succumbed to judgment, Satan would have
defeated him.

Paul's message to those who questioned
his qualification for ministry was to say:
"From now on let no person trouble me [by
making it necessary for me to vindicate my
apostolic authority and the divine truth of
my Gospel], for I bear on my body the
[brand] marks of the Lord Jesus [the
wounds, scars, and other outward evidence
of persecutions — these testify to His own-
ership of me]!" (Galatians 6:17).

Stand Your Ground

And the king assigned for them a
daily portion of his own rich and

dainty food and of the wine which he drank. They were to be so educated and so nourished for three years that at the end of that time they might stand before the king.

Daniel 1:5

After the fall of Judah to Babylon, Nebuchadnezzar, the king of Babylon at that time, decided to bring in some young Hebrew men and train them as his attendants. His purpose was to conform them to the lifestyle of his court.

But Daniel, one of the devout young men of Judah who loved the Lord, "...determined in his heart that he would not defile himself by [eating his portion of] the king's rich and dainty food or by [drinking] the wine which he drank..." (Daniel 1:8).

Daniel was determined he would be a Godpleaser and not a manpleaser. He refused to conform to the king's image of what he ought to be.

Daniel stood his ground and won favor with the king and his court. As a result of his fearless stand, God ended up using him in a very powerful way.

Exalted in the Kingdom

> Then the king made Daniel great and gave him many great gifts, and he made him to rule over the whole province of Babylon and to be chief governor over all the wise men of Babylon.

Daniel 2:48

Daniel went through a period of testing and trial, but, in the end, the same king who tried to get him to conform had such respect for him that he exalted him to a high position in the kingdom.

The same thing happened to me years ago in the work world. My boss wanted me, in a roundabout way, to help him steal some money. I was a bookkeeper, and he wanted me to write off a customer's credit balance. The customer had paid a bill twice, and my employer didn't want that fact reflected on the client's statement.

I refused to do it.

Some years down the road, I ended up having great favor in that company. I was made second in command in charge of the office, the warehouse, all the inventory, and all the truck drivers. I was called upon to solve problems I didn't even understand.

As a young woman I had a major position of leadership in the company. I didn't really have the education or even the training for the position.

How did that happen? It came about because, like Daniel, I refused to conform to a lower standard. I was respected in the company and was exalted to a high position of honor.

Those who try to get you to conform will not respect you if you do conform. In fact, they will despise your weakness. They will know they are controlling you and that what they are doing is wrong. But if you will stand your ground, you will be the one who ends up with the respect. For a while they may treat you as though you were the lowest life on earth. But when all is said and done, you will gain their respect.

Obey God

> [Then] Nebuchadnezzar said to them, Is it true, O Shadrach, Meshach, and Abednego, that you do not serve my gods or worship the golden image which I have set up?
>
> *Daniel 3:14*

This same king made a new rule and issued a new decree. He set up a golden image in the middle of the town and everybody was required to bow down before it and worship it. Anybody who refused to do so would be thrown into a fiery furnace.

Shadrach, Meshach and Abednego, three of Daniel's close friends, refused to bow down. They had the same Spirit on them that

Daniel did. The king said to them, "If you don't do as I say, I'm going to burn you alive."

Isn't that basically what the world says to you and me? If we refuse to conform to its standards, the world threatens us by saying, "If you do not bow down and do what we want you to do, if you do not fit into our mold, we are going to burn you alive."

That's when we need to do as the Hebrew children and trust the Lord.

Trust God

Shadrach, Meshach, and Abednego answered the king, O Nebuchadnezzar, it is not necessary for us to answer you on this point.

If our God Whom we serve is able to deliver us from the burning fiery furnace, He will deliver us out of your hand, O king.

But if not, let it be known to you, O king, that we will not serve your

gods or worship the golden image
which you have set up!

Daniel 3:16-18

Do you know what I like about Shadrach,
Meshach and Abednego? Their absolute
refusal to be frightened or intimidated. They
told the king: "We believe God is going to
deliver us, but even if He *doesn't,* we're not
conforming to your image of what you think
we ought to be. We're going to do what God
is telling us to do. You can do what you want
to with your furnace. But whatever happens
to us, we will have peace."

That is the attitude we ought to have
toward those who would try to pressure us
into disobeying what we know to be the will
of God for us.

Boldly Do What God Has Commanded

Now when Daniel knew that the
writing was signed, he went into his
house, and his windows being open

in his chamber toward Jerusalem,
he got down upon his knees three
times a day and prayed and gave
thanks before his God, as he had
done previously.

Daniel 6:10

Here is one final example from the book
of Daniel.

Later on another royal decree was issued
forbidding anyone to pray to anyone but the
king. The law was a trick used by Daniel's
enemies to try to destroy him. But Daniel
boldly went into his room and prayed to the
Lord with the windows open toward
Jerusalem just as he did every day.

If that had happened to us, would we have
closed the windows hoping not to get
caught? Would we have closed the windows
and just prayed once? Would we have done
just enough to hope God would not get mad
at us? Would we have tried to please both
God and the king?

If we believe we are doing the will of God, and we run into opposition, we need to boldly continue doing what we know God has told us to do.

Dare To Be Different

> So this [man] Daniel prospered in
> the reign of Darius and in the reign
> of Cyrus the Persian.
>
> *Daniel 6:28*

In every single account of Daniel, we find he was pressured to conform to what others wanted him to do and to be. He refused to yield to pressure. After a period of trial and tribulation, God exalted him and he was put in charge of the entire kingdom.

Have the courage to be different. It will change your life, and God will exalt you in the process.

7

❧

Learn To Cope With Criticism

If you are going to overcome insecurity, you are going to have to *learn to cope with criticism.*

Be Led by the Holy Spirit

But you have received the Holy Spirit and he lives within you, in your hearts, so that you don't need anyone to teach you what is right. For he teaches you all things, and he is the Truth....

1 John 2:27 TLB

Are you a self-validating person or do you need outside validation? By outside validation I mean somebody to tell you that you are okay, that what you are doing is all right. By self-validation, or inward validation, I mean taking action as you are led by the Holy Ghost, doing what you believe God is telling you to do.

One day I decided to redecorate my house. I got books of wallpaper samples and picked out patterns I thought would really look good, then showed them to other people and said, "I'm going to put this here and this here and this here. What do you think?"

Because I was insecure in that area I was looking for outside validation. I needed to hear what everybody thought about what I was doing.

Well, I didn't find one person who thought what I thought. Everyone I asked had a different opinion. Confusion came over me, and I hardly knew what to do.

We are all different; we are all individuals. I should not have expected anyone else to like what I liked. The real issue was whether I was satisfied with the outcome. I was the one who was going to have to live with it.

Don't waste your time asking other people whether your clothes are all right or whether your hair is okay or if they like your car. Become self-validating.

Make Your Own Decisions

But when it pleased God, who separated me from my mother's womb, and called me by his grace,

To reveal his Son in me, that I might preach him among the heathen; immediately I conferred not with flesh and blood.

Galatians 1:15,16 KJV

Paul said when he was called by God to preach the Gospel to the Gentiles, he did not confer with anyone else about the matter.

Many times when we receive a message from God, we confer too much with flesh and blood. We go around looking for someone to assure us we are doing the right thing. John tells us that since we have the Holy Spirit, the

Spirit of Truth, within us, we have no need to consult with other human beings.

Of course, there is another side to this question. The writer of Proverbs says that "...in the multitude of counselors there is safety" (Proverbs 11:14).

The answer is to be obedient to the Spirit without refusing counsel from others who are wiser or more knowledgeable about the subject than we are.

By listening to what people said to me about decorating, I learned some valuable principles, things I didn't even know before. But I did not let their opinions determine my final decision.

We must not allow ourselves to be unduly influenced by others simply because we are afraid to make our own decisions. If we are going to be self-validating people, we must learn to cope with criticism.

What if I had decorated my whole house according to the opinions of others and then someone else had come in and said, "Oh, I don't think I would have done it this way"? I would have been caught in a dilemma.

Some people seem to think it is their job in life to give their personal opinion on everything to everybody. One of the greatest lessons we can learn is not to offer — or receive — unsolicited opinions or advice.

Don't Come Under Bondage

> Stand fast therefore in the liberty wherewith Christ hath made us free, and be not entangled again with the yoke of bondage.

> *Galatians 5:1 KJV*

Be secure enough to know how to cope with criticism without feeling there is something wrong with you. Don't come under bondage thinking you have to conform to other people's opinions.

Suppose someone came into my newly re-decorated house and said to me, "You know,

I don't know if you're aware of this or not, Joyce, but if you put that flower arrangement on a little bit taller table, it would look better than it does on that shorter table."

If I were secure in myself and my own viewpoint, I could listen to that person's opinion without feeling I had to do what she suggested. If I had some humility about me, I could at least consider what she said.

"You know, I think you're right."

Sometimes I know something doesn't look right, but I don't know how to fix it. If someone who knows more about it has a suggestion, I can say, "Yes, I think you may be right; I'll try it."

Have enough confidence in who you are in Christ that you can listen to others and be open to change without feeling you have to agree with their viewpoint or meet with their approval if you don't feel their suggestion is right for you.

Learn to cope with criticism.

8

⚘

Determine Your Own Worth

Determine your own worth — don't let other people do it for you.

The Need for Affirmation

...You are My Beloved Son; in You
I am well pleased.

Mark 1:11

A child needs affirmation from his parents. It is the job of parents to teach their children they are loved despite their weaknesses and flaws.

If children are instilled with that knowledge from a young age, they will grow up with solidity to their personality. They will not always be on a "works trip" trying to manifest perfection, thinking that the only way they will be accepted is by their good deeds.

A lot of times parents don't know how to give that affirmation. Often they have problems because they did not receive affirmation from *their* parents.

I read a story about a man who had never been able to get affirmation from his father. The father had never said, "I love you and am pleased with you."

This man was successful, yet he was very unhappy and would find himself weeping and crying for no apparent reason. So he began to go to therapy where he discovered the root cause of his problem. He learned he was constantly trying to prove himself to his father through works, which left him worn out all the time.

Several times during these counseling sessions this man made trips across the country to his father's house still trying to get his father to affirm him. He longed to hear his father say, "Son, I love you and think you're great. I'm proud of what you've accomplished in life."

So many times we just want somebody to say, "I'm proud of you. I'm pleased with you." But sometimes we must come to realize we may never receive that affirmation we desire from certain people.

One day the man left his father's house saying to himself, "My father is never going to give me what I'm trying to get him to give me — he doesn't know how." When he said that, it was as though something broke in him. From that moment on he experienced a liberty of spirit he had never known before.

Accepted in the Beloved

For He foreordained us (destined us, planned in love for us) to be adopted (revealed) as His own children through Jesus Christ, in accordance with the purpose of His will [because it pleased Him and was His kind intent] —

[So that we might be] to the praise and the commendation of His glorious grace (favor and mercy), which He so freely bestowed on us in the Beloved.

Ephesians 1:5,6

Part of our struggle may simply be trying to get affirmation from somebody who is never going to give it to us because he simply doesn't know how.

The Bible teaches us that we have been made acceptable to God in the Beloved (His Son Jesus Christ), and that anyone who comes to the Father through Jesus He will in no wise cast out. (Ephesians 1:6 KJV; John 6:37 KJV.)

We need certain things from our loved ones, but if they do not know how to give those things to us, God does. He will be our mother, our father, our husband or wife, whatever we need Him to be.

The Lord will give us and build in us those things that others are not able to give us.

Take Responsibility for Your Own Actions

> And so each of us shall give an account of himself [give an answer in reference to judgment] to God.
>
> *Romans 14:12*

In the earlier years of my marriage I had many problems in my life and in my personality. After several years of marriage, Dave said to me, "You know what? If I determined my worth and my manhood by the way you treat me, I sure wouldn't have a very good opinion of myself."

Is there someone in your life you are not treating right? Are you trying to blame that person for your own faults? Is there someone who is making you miserable because of his own failure or unhappiness?

A woman in Chicago told me of her husband's arrest for public indecency.

"I can forgive him for that," she said. "He got caught up in pornography, and I know what a trap that is. But the one thing that I'm having a hard time with is, he's blaming it on me. He says he did it because I didn't meet his needs."

I told her, "Even if you weren't 'meeting his needs,' that's no excuse for his sin. You can't let somebody else put his problems off on you."

Often people who have problems don't want to take the responsibility for those problems. They look for a scapegoat. They look for somebody to blame.

I used to do that to my own family. Everything I did wrong was somebody else's fault: If Dave hadn't done a particular thing, I wouldn't have acted in a particular manner; if my kids helped me more in the house, I wouldn't complain all the time; if Dave didn't watch so much football, I wouldn't be constantly on his case. I always found a way to blame someone else for my negative attitude and behavior.

I am so glad my husband was secure in who he was in Christ. I am so glad he had a firm spiritual foundation and was able to love me through that period of time. I am so glad he refused to let me make him feel guilty or unhappy.

Our Worth Is Based on the Blood

> ...To Him Who ever loves us and has once [for all] loosed and freed us from our sins by His own blood.
>
> *Revelation 1:5*

We need to come to the place where we are secure enough in who we are in Christ that we will not allow our sense of worth to be based on the opinions or actions of others.

Don't try to find your worth in how you look. Don't try to find your worth in what you do. Don't try to find your worth in how other people treat you. You are worth something because Jesus shed His blood for you.

You may have faults, there may be things about you that need to be changed, but God is working on you the same as He is on everybody else. Don't let somebody else dump his problems off on you. Don't allow someone else to make you feel worthless or useless just because he doesn't know how to treat you right and love you as you deserve to be loved as a blood-bought child of God.

Recognize What Is Right With You

I have been crucified with Christ [in Him I have shared His crucifixion]; it is no longer I who live, but Christ (the Messiah) lives in me; and the life I now live in the body I live by faith in (by adherence to and reliance on and complete trust in) the

Son of God, Who loved me and gave
Himself up for me.

Galatians 2:20

God wants us to stop thinking all the time,
"What's wrong with me?" He wants us to
dwell on what is *right* with us.

Certainly we should recognize our faults
and weaknesses. We need to keep those areas
open before God all the time. We need to
confess, "Father, I know I'm not perfect; I
know I have faults and weaknesses. I want You
to work with me and change me. Show me my
faults and help me to overcome them, Lord."

But we must not let other people grind us
into the ground because of *their* weaknesses
and problems.

Don't spend all your life trying to win
somebody else's acceptance or approval.
Remember that you have already been
accepted and approved by God. Make sure
that your affirmation, your validation, your
sense of self-worth come from Him.

9

≈

Keep Your Flaws in Perspective

If you are ever going to really succeed at being yourself, you must *keep your flaws in perspective.*

Don't Focus on Imperfections

> ...look not to the things that are seen
> but to the things that are unseen....
>
> *2 Corinthians 4:18*

My secretary Roxane is very attractive. She has light blonde hair and beautiful cream-colored skin. If she even gets the least bit embarrassed her cheeks turn bright rosy red. She is one of those people who will probably still look twenty years old when she is forty. She is tiny (she weighs ninety-three pounds), yet she is not skinny. She is just really cute.

Roxane told me she went through years and years of major frustration about her body. In particular she thought her thighs were too big. She said she was so paranoid about them, she wouldn't wear certain kinds of clothes. She hardly ever wore a bathing suit.

I went out with her a couple of times to buy clothes. She would try on things that looked darling on her, but I could tell she was not happy with them. Finally she shared with me how uncomfortable she was about her thighs.

I couldn't believe it! When a person weighs ninety-three pounds, *nothing* can be too big!

I use that as an example because no matter how good we look, the devil will have us find some part of our body that we happen to think is imperfect, and he will cause us to focus on that one part even though we may be the only one who notices it.

I had my hair done one time and it wasn't cut in the back exactly the way I like it. No one else noticed that my hair looked any different. As a matter of fact, when I mentioned it to Dave, he said, "You know that's really funny because I've been thinking the last few days how nice the back of your hair has looked recently."

It's just a matter of getting our eyes off the one imperfection and looking at everything in perspective.

If we are ever going to overcome feeling insecure about ourselves, we must learn to put our flaws into perspective. All of us have flaws, but we don't have to stare at them in the mirror twenty-four hours a day.

If we told our closest friends some of the things we think are flaws, they would probably just laugh at us. In fact, they might think those things we consider to be our greatest flaws are some of our best qualities.

Be Satisfied With Your Looks

> ...Will what is formed say to him that formed it, Why have you made me thus?
>
> *Romans 9:20*

The devil puts such junk in our minds. Who decides what a perfect body is anyway? Who draws out the model and says, "Now everybody who doesn't look like this is wrong?"

God created every one of us. According to Ephesians 2:10 we are His own handiwork, His workmanship. Therefore, He must like what He has made. To be pleasing to God we don't all have to look like a fashion model or a muscle man!

Each one of us has to come to a place where we are satisfied with how we look. That doesn't mean we don't need to exercise or perhaps lose some weight. I am not talking about making an effort to stay trim and healthy. I am talking about all these foolish things we get caught up in, things that so often we cannot change about ourselves.

Do you want to overcome insecurity in your life? Learn to keep your flaws in perspective.

10

❧

Discover the True
Source of Confidence

The final and most important step to
becoming more secure is to *discover the true
source of confidence.*

Put No Confidence in the Flesh

For we [Christians] are the true
circumcision, who worship God in
spirit and by the Spirit of God and
exult and glory and pride ourselves
in Jesus Christ, and put no confidence or dependence [on what we
are] in the flesh and on outward priv-
ileges and physical advantages and
external appearances.

Philippians 3:3

In what do you place your confidence? That question must be settled before you can ever have God's confidence. Before your confidence can be in Him, you must remove your confidence from other things.

Don't place your confidence in the flesh — in appearance, education, finances, position or relationship.

One time my daughter Sandy and her boyfriend broke up. I told her, "That's a shame, he really lost out."

If somebody doesn't want to have a relationship with you, why do you feel you are the one to blame? Maybe the other person is the one who is at fault.

If the devil thinks he can get you on the run with negative thoughts, he will chase you around from now until Jesus comes. Sooner or later you must come to the place where your confidence is not in the flesh or outward appearance but in Christ Jesus.

A young woman told me how much value she placed in her grades at school. She had a learning disability similar to dyslexia, and she studied hard so that nobody could tell from her grades that she had a problem. But she was studying *so* hard it was actually stealing her joy.

I told her, "You need to put those grades on the altar." I watched as fear came all over her.

"My grades really mean a lot to me," she said. "Not a little bit, but a lot."

Her real problem was not her learning disability, it was her confidence disability. She was trusting in grades rather than in God.

I have seen my daughter try so hard to get her hair to look good that I was surprised she had hair left when she was done. Sometimes her hair would look better *before* she combed it than it did after she had spent an hour fussing with it. But in her mind she could not face the world unless every hair was in its place.

That is another example of misplaced confidence.

Misplaced Confidence

For the Lord shall be your confidence, firm and strong....

Proverbs 3:26

Parents sometimes place their confidence in the accomplishments of their children, which can sometimes lead to serious problems for both of them. One father, for example, wanted his daughter to be a doctor, so she began to value her worth in terms of that goal. What her father did not know was that God had already picked his daughter to be my secretary!

Is God dealing with you about where you have placed your confidence? Is it in marriage? A college degree? Your job? Your spouse? Your children?

As Christians, we should not place our confidence in our education, our looks, our position, our property, our gifts, our talents, our abilities, our accomplishments or in other people's opinions. Our heavenly Father is saying to us, "No more; it is time to let go of all those fleshly things to which you have been holding so firmly so long. It is time to put your trust and confidence in Me, and Me alone!"

But too often, like some of the Old Testament prophets, we allow ourselves to be influenced by what others think and say, and by how they look.

You Are What God Says You Are

Then the word of the Lord came to me [Jeremiah], saying,

Before I formed you in the womb I knew and approved of you [as My chosen instrument], and before you were born I separated and set you apart, consecrating you; [and] I appointed you as a prophet to the nations.

Then said I, Ah, Lord God! Behold,
I cannot speak, for I am only a youth.

But the Lord said to me, Say not, I
am only a youth; for you shall go to all
to whom I shall send you, and whatever I command you, you shall speak.

Be not afraid of them [their faces],
for I am with you to deliver you,
says the Lord.

Jeremiah 1:4-8

Jeremiah was afraid to preach. He said, "I
cannot speak." God said, "You get out there
and do what I tell you to do. Speak to the
people the message I give you. Don't look at
their faces. I am with you to deliver you
from all their wrath because you are My
chosen vessel."

If God says we are something, then we
are, whether anybody else agrees or not.

People told me I couldn't preach. Actually it was funny because they told me I
couldn't preach *after* I was already doing it!

Some people said, "You can't preach because you are a woman."

I said, "I can't?"

"No, you can't."

"But I am preaching," I said. "I already am!"

Certainly there were temptations to quit because of all the criticism I received. But I never gave in to those temptations because I knew I was doing what God had told me to do. Like Paul, I found my confidence in the Lord, not in religion.

Religion Can Interfere With God

Though for myself I have [at least grounds] to rely on the flesh. If any other man considers that he has or seems to have reason to rely on the flesh and his physical and outward advantages, I have still more!

Circumcised when I was eight days old, of the race of Israel, of the tribe of Benjamin, a Hebrew [and

the son] of Hebrews; as to the obser-
vance of the Law I was of [the party
of] the Pharisees,

As to my zeal, I was a persecutor
of the church, and by the Law's
standard of righteousness (supposed
justice, uprightness, and right standing with God) I was proven to be
blameless and no fault was found
with me.

Philippians 3:4-6

Paul was not only a Pharisee, perhaps the
most pious of the Jews of his day, he was a
chief of the Pharisees. He was so religious he
kept all of the stringent religious rules of his
sect. But he discovered that none of his religious piety mattered at all, so he was quite
willing to give it all up in order to gain Christ.

Give Up Rules for Christ

But whatever former things I had
that might have been gains to me, I

have come to consider as [one combined] loss for Christ's sake.

Yes, furthermore, I count everything as loss compared to the possession of the priceless privilege (the overwhelming preciousness, the surpassing worth, and supreme advantage) of knowing Christ Jesus my Lord and of progressively becoming more deeply and intimately acquainted with Him [of perceiving and recognizing and understanding Him more fully and clearly]. For His sake I have lost everything and consider it all to be mere rubbish (refuse, dregs), in order that I may win (gain) Christ (the Anointed One).

Philippians 3:7,8

What kind of rules are you trying to keep in order to find a sense of self-worth? Maybe your rules are praying a certain amount of time or reading so many chapters of the Bible each day.

Religious rules tell us, "Do this, do that, don't eat this, don't touch that." (Colossians 2:20,21.) But God wants us to do what Paul did — get rid of all those rules and regulations so we can gain Christ and be known and found in Him.

Be Found and Known in Christ

And that I may [actually] be found and known as in Him, not having any [self-achieved] righteousness that can be called my own, based on my obedience to the Law's demands (ritualistic uprightness and supposed right standing with God thus acquired), but possessing that [genuine righteousness] which comes through faith in Christ (the Anointed One), the [truly] right standing with

God, which comes from God by
[saving] faith.

Philippians 3:9

This verse has an anointing on it that must
not be missed. In it Paul says he wants to
achieve one thing in life — to be found and
known in Christ.

This needs to be our attitude also. We
cannot always manifest perfect *behavior,* but
with God's help we can always reflect a
perfect *Savior.*

Do you know why God will never let us
achieve perfect behavior? If we ever did, we
would derive our sense of worth from our
perfection and performance rather than from
His love and grace.

If you and I behaved perfectly all the
time, we would think God owed us an
answer to our prayers because of our obedience to all the rules and regulations. So do
you know what God does? He leaves us
some weaknesses so we have to go to Him

constantly to ask for His help — so we have to depend on Him whether we like it or not.

God is not going to let us work our way into a sense of peace and fulfillment. But He will allow us to work ourselves into a fit and frenzy. Why? So we will realize that works of the flesh produce nothing but misery and frustration. (Romans 3:20.)

If that is so, what are we supposed to do? Just relax and enjoy life. We need to learn to enjoy God more. That will not only help us, it will also take the pressure off the people around us. We need to quit demanding that everyone be perfect all the time. We need to start enjoying them just as they are.

In essence Paul said he wanted to be able to stand before God and say, "Well, here I am, Lord, as big a mess as ever! I don't have any good works to offer You; I don't have a perfect record; but I do believe in Jesus."

You and I have to live like that every day or we will never enjoy peace and contentment.

We cannot enjoy life if everything is based on our good works. We must learn to acknowledge our dependence on God.

Three Steps to Dependence on God

> Trust (lean on, rely on, and be confident) in the Lord and do good; so shall you dwell in the land and feed surely on His faithfulness, and truly you shall be fed.

> *Psalm 37:3*

There are three steps to a position of dependence on God.

First, learn what you are not. Accept the fact that you are not going to achieve success in life based upon your works. Instead, like it or not, you must trust God: "Commit your way to the Lord [roll and repose each care of your load on Him]; trust (lean on, rely on, and be confident) also in Him and He will bring it to pass" (Psalm 37:5).

The second step to staying in a position of dependence on God is to learn Who God is:

"To you it was shown, that you might realize and have personal knowledge that the Lord is God; there is no other besides Him" (Deuteronomy 4:35).

The third step is to learn that as God is so are you: "...we may have confidence... because as He is, so are we in this world" (1 John 4:17).

Not by Bread Alone

You shall [earnestly] remember all the way which the Lord your God led you these forty years in the wilderness, to humble you and to prove you, to know what was in your [mind and] heart, whether you would keep His commandments or not.

And He humbled you and allowed you to hunger and fed you with manna, which you did not know nor did your fathers know, that He might make you recognize and personally know that man does not live by

bread only, but man lives by every
word that proceeds out of the mouth
of the Lord.

Deuteronomy 8:2,3

I once went through a set of circumstances concerning my ministry that was
confusing and upsetting. On some days there
would be all kinds of mail and money for the
ministry. The next day I would go to the post
office and find only two or three pieces of
mail. One week I would have a meeting with
a large crowd, then the next week there
would only be half as many in attendance.
Satan would say to me, "Well, the people
didn't like what you said last week so they
didn't come back."

When circumstances conveyed to me I
was doing well, my emotions were up. When
circumstances indicated I was not doing very
well, my emotions were down. The devil had
me on the run. Every good experience elated

me; every bad circumstance deflated me. (I call this "yo-yo" Christianity.)

This situation went on for years. Dave would try to tell me I was just under attack from the devil, but I couldn't see it. I saw the situation with my head, but I did not understand it in my heart.

One day as I was driving in my hometown I said to God, "Why is this happening?" The Spirit of the Lord said to me, "I am teaching you that man does not live by bread alone, but by every word that proceeds out of the mouth of God."

Bread was the daily sustenance for the children of Israel. Bread kept them going. When the Lord spoke to me about bread, He was saying, "I am trying to teach you that you cannot live by all these other things that keep you going. You must look to Me for your daily strength."

After delivering them from their oppressors in Egypt, God kept the Israelites out in the wilderness for forty years teaching them that very lesson. They were slow learners. Deuteronomy 1:2 says, "It is [only] eleven days' journey from Horeb by the way of Mount Seir to Kadesh-barnea [on Canaan's border; yet Israel took forty years to get beyond it]."

God as Deliverer and Sustainer

He brought [Israel] forth also with silver and gold, and there was not one feeble person among their tribes.

Psalm 105:37

When the Israelites came out of Egypt, they were a blessed people. They had seen the miracles of God and all the things He had done to Pharaoh on their behalf. Because the Lord was with them, they came out of the land of bondage with much of the Egyptians' material wealth, and with great physical health and stamina.

But God wanted them to know that it was He Who brought them out, and not they themselves. He wanted them to learn if they were to stay out of trouble, they had to keep depending on Him.

I used to think the size of the crowds in my meetings was dependent on my good preaching. I did not yet understand that it was not Joyce Meyer who got the people to the meetings. I had to learn that if they came, God had to bring them. I had to learn total dependence on God. It took me almost forty years also. Hopefully reading this book will save you some time.

The Key to Joy and Peace in God

> And beware lest you say in your [mind and] heart, My power and the might of my hand have gotten me this wealth.

> *Deuteronomy 8:17*

I now realize my joy has to be in God, not in my ministry. My peace has to be in the Lord, not in my works.

Not everything that comes into our lives is from God. But God will use the things of life

— both bad and good — to teach us to depend upon Him.

I no longer have thoughts that bigger crowds are a result of my efforts. Now when I finish preaching I say, "Well, Lord, what happens next time will be up to You. You got the people here this time. If You want them to return, You will have to bring them back. I am just going to get up and preach the best I know how and leave the rest to You."

If you truly want to live in peace and security, that is the attitude you must have. You must do your best and then leave the results to God.

Allow the Lord to shake loose from you all those earthly things from which you are trying so hard to derive a sense of confidence, worth, security and well being. You may as well let Him have them, because He will not give up until He has His way — and His way is always best.

Conclusion

~≈~

It is so important to have a positive sense of self-esteem, self-value and self-worth, to be secure in who we are in Christ, to truly like ourselves. We learn to like ourselves by learning how much God loves us. Once we become rooted and grounded in God's love, we can come to terms of peace with ourselves.

Ten Steps to Building Confidence

Following is a list of the ten steps to building confidence. I urge you to copy it and put it up somewhere where you can see it every day.

1. Never speak negatively about yourself.

2. Celebrate the positive.

3. Avoid comparisons.

4. Focus on potential, not limitations.

5. Exercise your gift.

6. Have the courage to be different.

7. Learn to cope with criticism.

8. Determine your own worth.

9. Keep your flaws in perspective.

10. Discover the true Source of confidence.

Part 2

Scriptures

Scriptures
On Confidence

⤳

There is no fear in love; but perfect
love casts out fear, because fear
involves torment. But he who fears
has not been made perfect in love.

1 John 4:18 NKJV

Satan enjoys tormenting people in a
variety of ways. Insecurity, self-rejection,
self-punishment and a poor self-image are
some of his ways. Insecurity is nothing but a
diminished version of the spirit of fear.

Let these Scriptures minister the love of God
to you, and your insecurities will fade away.

For you are a holy and set-apart
people to the Lord your God; the
Lord your God has chosen you to be
a special people to Himself out of all
the peoples on the face of the earth.

The Lord did not set His love upon
you and choose you because you were

more in number than any other people,
for you were the fewest of all people.

Deuteronomy 7:6,7

And you shall be secure and feel
confident because there is hope; yes,
you shall search about you, and you
shall take your rest in safety.

You shall lie down, and none shall
make you afraid....

Job 11:18,19

You number and record my wan-
derings; put my tears into Your
bottle — are they not in Your book?

Psalm 56:8

For God so greatly loved and dearly
prized the world that He [even] gave
up His only begotten (unique) Son, so
that whoever believes in (trusts in,
clings to, relies on) Him shall not
perish (come to destruction, be lost)
but have eternal (everlasting) life.

John 3:16

...May you be rooted deep in love and founded securely on love,

That you may have the power and be strong to apprehend and grasp with all the saints [God's devoted people, the experience of that love] what is the breadth and length and height and depth [of it];

[That you may really come] to know [practically, through experience for yourselves] the love of Christ, which far surpasses mere knowledge [without experience]; that you may be filled [through all your being] unto all the fullness of God [may have the richest measure of the divine Presence, and become a body wholly filled and flooded with God Himself]!

Ephesians 3:17-19

For God did not give us a spirit of timidity (of cowardice, of craven and cringing and fawning fear), but [He has given us a spirit] of power and of love and of calm and well-balanced mind and discipline and self-control.

2 Timothy 1:7

...My trust and assured reliance and confident hope shall be fixed in Him....

Hebrews 2:13

And we know (understand, recognize, are conscious of, by observation and by experience) and believe (adhere to and put faith in and rely on) the love God cherishes for us. God is love, and he who dwells and continues in love dwells and continues in God, and God dwells and continues in him.

1 John 4:16

We love Him, because He first loved us.

1 John 4:19

Prayer for Confidence

Glorious Father,

I am made in Your own image, therefore I am not insecure. My security is in You. You are my righteousness and my peace.

I turn away from the fear of man and the feeling that I just don't measure up. Help me to stop comparing myself to others. Help me to see myself as You see me — complete, secure and whole. Help me to remember that through Christ Jesus I am able to overcome all of my insecurities and walk in quiet confidence all the days of my life!

In Jesus' name, amen!

Prayer for a
Personal Relationship
With the Lord

~❧~

If you have never invited Jesus, the Prince of Peace, to be your Lord and Savior, I invite you to do so now. Pray the following prayer, and if you are really sincere about it, you will experience a new life in Christ.

Father,

You loved the world so much, You gave Your only begotten Son to die for our sins so that whoever believes in Him will not perish, but have eternal life.

Your Word says we are saved by grace through faith as a gift from You. There is nothing we can do to earn salvation.

I believe and confess with my mouth that Jesus Christ is Your Son, the Savior of the world. I believe He died on the cross for me and bore all of my sins, paying the price for them. I believe in my heart that You raised Jesus from the dead.

I ask You to forgive my sins. I confess Jesus as my Lord. According to Your Word, I am saved and will spend eternity with You! Thank You, Father. I am so grateful! In Jesus' name, amen.

See John 3:16; Ephesians 2:8,9; Romans 10:9,10; 1 Corinthians 15:3,4; 1 John 1:9; 4:14-16; 5:1,12,13.

Endnotes

Chapter 4

[1]   Helen Hayes with Katherine Hatch, *My Life in Three Acts* (New York: Harcourt Brace Jovanovich, Publishers, 1990), pp. 39, 66.

[2]   Mary Kittredge, *Helen Hayes* (New York: Chelsea House Publishers, 1990), p. 64.

Chapter 6

[1]   *Webster's II New College Dictionary* (Boston/New York: Houghton Mifflin Company, 1995), s.v. "conform."

References

The *King James Version* of the Bible (KJV).

The Living Bible (TLB) © 1971. Used by permission of Tyndale House Publishers, Inc., Wheaton, Illinois 60189. All rights reserved.

The New King James Version (NKJV) of the Bible. Copyright © 1979, 1980, 1982 by Thomas Nelson, Inc., Publishers. Used by permission.

About the Author

∽

Joyce Meyer has been teaching the Word of God since 1976 and in full-time ministry since 1980. As an associate pastor at Life Christian Center in St. Louis, Missouri, she developed, coordinated and taught a weekly meeting known as "Life In The Word." After more than five years, the Lord brought it to a conclusion, directing her to establish her own ministry and call it "Life In The Word, Inc."

Joyce's "Life In The Word" radio broadcast is heard on over 250 stations nationwide. Joyce's 30-minute "Life In The Word With Joyce Meyer" television program was released in 1993 and is broadcast throughout the United States and several foreign countries. Her teaching tapes are enjoyed internationally. She travels extensively conducting Life In The Word conferences, as well as speaking in local churches.

Joyce and her husband, Dave, business administrator at Life In The Word, have been married for 31 years and are the parents of four children. Three are married, and their youngest son resides with them in Fenton, Missouri, a St. Louis suburb.

Joyce believes the call on her life is to establish believers in God's Word. She says, "Jesus died to set the captives free, and far too many Christians have little or no victory in their daily lives." Finding herself in the same situation many years ago, and having found freedom to live in victory through applying God's Word, Joyce goes equipped to set captives free and to exchange *ashes for beauty*.

Joyce has taught on emotional healing and related subjects in meetings all over the country, helping multiplied thousands. She has recorded over 170 different audio cassette albums and is the author of 25 books to help the Body of Christ on various topics.

Her "Emotional Healing Package" contains over 23 hours of teaching on the subject. Albums included in this package are:

"Confidence"; "Beauty for Ashes" (includes a syllabus); "Managing Your Emotions"; "Bitterness, Resentment, and Unforgiveness"; "Root of Rejection"; and a 90-minute Scripture/music tape entitled, "Healing the Brokenhearted."

Joyce's "Mind Package" features five different audio tape series on the subject of the mind. They include: "Mental Strongholds and Mindsets"; "Wilderness Mentality"; "The Mind of the Flesh"; "The Wandering, Wondering Mind"; and "Mind, Mouth, Moods & Attitudes." The package also contains Joyce's powerful 260-page book, *Battlefield of the Mind*. On the subject of love she has two tape series entitled, "Love Is..." and "Love: The Ultimate Power."

Write to Joyce Meyer's office for a resource catalog and further information on how to obtain the tapes you need to bring total healing to your life.

To contact the author write: Joyce Meyer
Life In The Word, Inc. • P. O. Box 655
Fenton, Missouri 63026
or call: (314) 349-0303

*Please include your testimony
or help received from this
book when you write.
Your prayer requests are welcome.*

In Canada, please write:
Joyce Meyer Ministries Canada, Inc.
P. O. Box 2995 • London, ON N6A 4H9

In Australia, please write:
Joyce Meyer Ministries-Australia
Locked Bag 77 • Mansfield Delivery Centre
Queensland 4122
or call: (07) 3349 1200

❧

The Harrison House Vision

Proclaiming the truth and the power
Of the Gospel of Jesus Christ
With excellence;

Challenging Christians to
Live victoriously,
Grow spiritually,
Know God intimately.